Camping Cookbook

Hobo Pie Iron Recipes

Louise Davidson

Efforts were made to ensure that the information in this book is accurate and complete. However, the author and the publisher do not warrant the accuracy of the information, text, and graphics contained within the book due to the rapidly changing nature of science, research, known and unknown facts, and the internet. The author and the publisher do not hold any responsibility for errors, omissions, or contrary interpretation of the subject matter herein. This book is presented solely for motivational and informational purposes.

The recipes provided in this book are for informational purposes only and are not intended to provide dietary advice. A medical practitioner should be consulted before making any changes in diet. Additionally, recipes' cooking times may require adjustment depending on age and quality of appliances. Readers are strongly urged to take all precautions to ensure ingredients are fully cooked to avoid the dangers of foodborne illnesses. The recipes and suggestions provided in this book are solely the opinions of the author. The author and publisher do not take any responsibility for any consequences that may result due to following the instructions provided in this book. The nutritional information for recipes contained in this book are provided for informational purposes only. This information is based on the specific brands, ingredients, and measurements used to make the recipe, and therefore the nutritional information is an estimate, and in no way is intended to be a guarantee of the actual nutritional value of the recipe made in the reader's home. The author and the publisher will not be responsible for any damages resulting in your reliance on the nutritional information. The best method to obtain an accurate count of the nutritional value in the recipe is to calculate the information with your specific brands, ingredients, and measurements.

ISBN: 9798669385231

Printed in the United States

www.thecookbookpublisher.com/

CONTENTS

INTRODUCTION

Admit it—don't you get tired of eating s'mores and hot dogs by the second day of camping? Camping trips are all about getting out of the routine, but it just doesn't seem like an adventure when you have to eat the same food over and over; it feels more like an obligation. Before you know it, you suddenly start to miss all those delicious favorite meals that you can cook anytime at home.

Fortunately, enough, there is a way you can relax with friends and family in the great outdoors and still have fun with your favorite foods. It's called a pie iron, and what it is, is a compact, sturdy container made of pre-seasoned cast iron or aluminum with long handles that lets you cook your food directly over the campfire. Pie irons are also known as camp iron pie, pudgy pie, mountain pie or hobo pie

When you are camping in the wilderness, the pie iron becomes your best friend for preparing a wide variety of popular campfire recipes. With a smart selection of ingredients and a little imagination, you can grill, bake, and roast to savor your favorite meals using only this small pan.

The pie iron is sometimes known as a "sandwich maker," but it's useful for much more than just cooking sandwiches. Be it breakfast buns, waffles, omelets, cinnamon rolls, pies, pizzas, wraps, fajitas, cookies—and yes, sandwiches—its simple design lets you cook a variety of meals in just a few minutes over the campfire coals. And with only two surfaces in contact with the food, it's also easy to clean up after you're done cooking.

Looking for inspiring food ideas for your next camping trip? This book presents 50 easy and delicious hobo pie iron recipes to try. These filling, mouthwatering recipes will transform your camping trip into an amazing food trip as you create lifelong memories with your family and friends in the company of these campfire cast-iron hobo pie meals.

It's time to take your campfire gustation to the next level. Get creative and prepare some delicious and filling meals to make the most out of your next camping trip.

In the next section, we discuss food safety at the campsite, what to bring on your planning a successful camping trip, and cooking tips.

Safety around the Fire and Cooking in the Outdoors

Much of the cooking within this book refers to the open-flame style of cooking.
Fire safety is essential. Always keep an eye on the fire, never leave it unattended, and make sure that the fire is completely out, even if it is in a fire ring. Keep fire extinguishers at the ready, just in case.

Second, fire cooking is a tricky business. Until you know how to judge the heat of a fire or its coals, you may have some challenges first. The best way to attain success is to keep vigilant while cooking. Note that the best way to cook is directly on hot coals. This means you must have the time to start a fire, make it hot, and then let it die down into coals. If you do not have this time or patience, you might want to consider alternatives, as cooking over a flame though good, is trickier. Using a grill is helpful, and moving the food consistently may help prevent scorching. If you do not feel comfortable cooking over an open flame, any camp stove will work quite well.

Do not forget to put the fire out after you are finished using it. One of the best ways to do this is to cover it with sand or dirt until it dies off completely.

Here are some additional tips regarding food safety. While this list is by no means exhaustive, it is a good starting point.

- Washing your hands before and after handling food is an important safety rule to follow at all times. It may be even more so when cooking outside. You can also use hand sanitizers.
- Working on a clean surface, and keeping bugs and undesired creepy crawlers out of your food supply is also vital to avoid food poisoning. If you can, keeping your cooler in your car or trailer is a really good way to avoid contamination.
- Wash your fruits and vegetables with safe, drinkable water.
- Drink bottle you've bought or brought from home to make sure the water supply you use is safe to drink.
- Clean-up immediately after each meal, storing leftover food in airtight containers and away from night prowlers.

Food Security

All that said, special care should be taken when preparing your foods on site. Many of these recipes include foods that require refrigeration. Keep all foods in a cooler filled with ice or in a refrigerator until cooking. This is especially true for raw meats, dairy, and eggs. When preparing raw meats (and eggs), be careful not to cross-contaminate. This is when raw meat juices spread to other foods, like vegetables, which may be left raw. This is a problem because botulism and other bacteria can cause serious illness when consumed, even in small quantities. Make sure to wash hands, knives, and prep materials between each dish. Keeping a cutting board and knives for each food item (green for vegetables, white for meat, for example) can help prevent cross-contamination. You may wish to prepare as much as possible before your camping trip.

Some Essentials to Bring on Your Trip

For the fire
Waterproof matches or a few good lighters
Starter liquid fluid
Starter wood
Charcoals (plenty of it)
Cooking utensils for barbecue tongs, spatula, extra-long forks, cleaning brush for the grill.
Grill (for over the fire, if the campsite does not provide or you like having your own)
A grate to place directly on the fire to cook food on the open flame

To prepare and cook the food
Pie irons, cast iron is preferable for even cooking and durability.
Large cast-iron skillet or metal skillet that can be placed on the grill or fire
Saucepan
Heavy-duty aluminum foil
A cooking spray of your choice.
Olive oil, butter
Salt and pepper and other seasonings you may want to use, like garlic powder, chili powder, and other spices.
Oven mitts (preferably silicone to accommodate very high temperatures)
Can opener
Bottle opener
Prepping knives, cutting board
Whisk, spoons, wooden spoon, slotted spoon
Grater, vegetable peeler
Plastic strainer
Large unbreakable serving plates
Mixing bowl, various size
Measuring cups and spoons
Wood skewers

Ziplock bags

Mason jars – great for mixing dressings and has many other uses

To keep the food
One cooler with plenty of ice or ice packs to keep perishable food and drinks fresh
A second cooler or large plastic covered bin for a dry non-perishable item like cans, pasta, rice, cereals, seasoning, and spices.
Plastic wrap
Plastic airtight containers for food leftover storage

To eat
Non-breakable plates, glass, cups, mugs, utensils
Napkins
Plastic tablecloth
Water bottles

To clean-up
Paper towels
Washing clothes, drying clothes
Dishwashing tub, dishwashing soap

Prep Early to Make Camping More Fun

You can make cooking at the campsite even easier on yourself by doing some of the food prep at home. Plastic food storage bags with secure closures are great for carrying premade ingredients in. They can be washable or disposable depending on your preference, they can easily be labeled, and they are the most compact way of storing food in small spaces.

When preparing food at home for the campsite, you have a couple of different options. With some dishes, you can prepare all of the ingredients and combine them together in one container so that all you need to do is transfer them from the container they will be cooked in. If you find that many of the dishes that you plan on preparing to use the same ingredients, you can prepare larger quantities of those ingredients and store them in a plastic bag, retrieving only what you need at any given time. You can also prepare each set of ingredients for dishes separately, bag and label it, and then assemble it at the campsite.

When camping, you don't have to give up homemade flavor in favor of convenience foods. However certain premade, canned, and frozen foods not only save you time but can also be easily enhanced with just a few small additions. For example, a jarred sauce with the addition of a few spices will taste heavenly and save you the extra time and ingredients of creating it from scratch.

Always pack a little extra. You never know when you will want seconds or meet a new mouth to feed. Welcome others into your campsite and make new friends and memories around your cast iron Dutch oven.

Campsite Cooking Hacks

Listed below are some campsite cooking hacks that are not only innovative but very effective.

- Store dry herbs and spices in old Tic Tac® boxes.
- Aluminum foil is the best way to pack food because you can cook it over the fire during camping. Do remember to bring lots with you!
- If possible, bring along a Dutch oven. Using this, you can try countless delicious recipes for everything from pizza and cakes to soups and stews.
- You can make an omelet by boiling it in a Ziploc® bag until the eggs are set.
- Precooking bacon or sausages at home save a lot of time and mess at the campsite.
- Before leaving home, clean empty condiment bottles and fill them with pancake batter, cake batter, or premixed omelets to take along with you for an easy meal.
- When you open the packets, be careful of the hot steam escaping. Do not allow small children to open hot packets.

BREAKFAST

Egg Nest

Make the most of your morning camp routine with this energizing egg nest. It is loaded with filling and nutritious eggs and potatoes to keep you going till lunchtime.

Serves 1 - Prep. time 5 minutes
Cooking time 5–10 minutes

Ingredients
½ cup hash brown potatoes
¼ teaspoon onion powder
1 tablespoon butter or oil
Pinch of paprika
1 egg
Dash of salt and pepper

Directions
1. Prepare the campfire.
2. Grease both sides of the pie iron with some butter or vegetable oil.
3. Add the potatoes, onion powder, and 1 tablespoon of butter or oil.
4. Close and latch the pie iron.
5. Place the pie iron over the coals and cook until the potatoes begin to brown.
6. Remove the pie iron from the coals. Use a fork to create a nest-like hollow in the center of the potatoes. Break the egg into the hollow. Top with paprika, salt, and pepper.
7. Close the pie iron and cook until the eggs are cooked well and the potatoes are browned.
8. Remove the pie iron from the coals. Serve warm.

Nutrition Facts per Serving
Calories 375, total fat 25.7 g, carb 28.4 g,
Protein 8.1 g, sodium 411 mg

Sausage Breakfast Sandwich

After a chilly night in your tent, this healthy, warming sausage sandwich is all you need for a truly good campfire morning. Enjoy the triple combination of eggs, cheese, and sausage along with a mug of hot coffee for a complete breakfast experience.

Serves 6 - Prep. time 8–10 minutes
Cooking time 5–10 minutes

Ingredients
6 eggs
6 slices sharp cheddar
6 defrosted vegetarian sausages (or pre-cooked sausages)
12 slices sandwich bread

Directions
1. Prepare the campfire.
2. Preheat the pie iron and grease both sides with butter.
3. Lightly beat the eggs.
4. Add bread slices on both sides of the pie iron. Press gently in the middle to create space for the filling.
5. Pour egg in the filling space on one side and top with cheese.
6. Place a sausage over the other bread slice.
7. Close and latch the pie iron.
8. Place the pie iron over the coals and cook until the cheese melts and the egg is set.
9. Remove the pie iron from the coals. Repeat the above steps to prepare the remaining sandwiches.
10. Serve warm.

Nutrition Facts per Serving
Calories 425, total fat 17.7 g, carb 38.9 g,
Protein 28.7 g, sodium 853 mg

Ham and Egg Sandwich

This ham and egg sandwich is full of baked goodness, which makes it one of the most popular campfire breakfast recipes. This sandwich requires minimal preparation and delivers maximum satisfaction. You can use a skillet to fry the eggs to your satisfaction.

Serves 1 - Prep. time 5 minutes
Cooking time 10 minutes

Ingredients
1 sliced ham
1 egg, fried
2 slices of loaf bread
1 slice cheddar cheese
Butter or margarine (optional)

Directions
1. Prepare the campfire.
2. Grease both sides of the pie iron with butter, vegetable oil, or cooking spray.
3. Add one bread piece and top with cheese, ham, and eggs.
4. Place another bread piece on top.
5. Close and latch the pie iron.
6. Place the pie iron over the coals and cook for about 10–12 minutes total, rotating after 5–6 minutes, until the bread is evenly brown.
7. Remove the pie iron from the coals. Serve warm.

Nutrition Facts per Serving
Calories 393, total fat 21.5 g, carb 27.3 g,
Protein 21.7 g, sodium 1036 mg

Cheesy Ham Omelet

After a cozy night in camp, it does take a bit of effort to get out of your sleeping bag. However, just the thought of savoring this amazing breakfast omelet will make you jump out of your tent right away. This protein-rich breakfast will get you moving and will make you want to have it again the next morning.

Serves 4 - Prep. time 5 minutes
Cooking time 5 minutes

Ingredients
½ pound carving board ham, chopped
5 eggs, scrambled
½ red pepper, diced
½ green pepper, diced
½ onion, diced
½ cup shredded cheese
2 packages crescent rolls
Mushrooms (optional)

Directions
1. Prepare the campfire.
2. Take a skillet, add some oil or butter, and crack the eggs into it. Cook until scrambled.
3. Grease both sides of the pie iron with butter, vegetable oil, or cooking spray.
4. Place two crescent rolls on one side.
5. Add the scrambled eggs and top with the ham, veggies, and cheese.
6. Place two more crescent rolls on top. Pinch the sides to make a seal.
7. Place the pie iron over the coals and cook for about 4 minutes total, rotating after 2 minutes, until evenly brown.
8. Remove the pie iron from the coals. Serve warm.

Nutrition Facts per Serving
Calories 198, total fat 11.3 g, carb 11 g,
Protein 13.4 g, sodium 312 mg

Bacon Veggie Sandwich

One nice thing about this sandwich is that you can prepare your choice of assorted veggies in advance before leaving home. You don't have to, of course, as you can always prepare them at the campsite, but it saves time and is more convenient. You don't have to use whole wheat bread, either—you can choose any bread you wish, be it multi-grain, white bread, or whatever.

Serves 4 - Prep. time 15–20 minutes
Cooking time 10 minutes

Ingredients
8 strips bacon
8 slices whole-wheat bread
Assorted veggies (green onions, avocado, peppers, mushrooms, tomatoes, etc.)
1 cups shredded cheese
4 eggs, scrambled

Directions
1. Prepare the campfire.
2. Preheat the pie iron and grease both sides with butter, vegetable oil, or cooking spray.
3. Add some oil or butter to a skillet and crack the eggs into it. Cook until scrambled. Set aside.
4. Add the bacon to the skillet and cook on both sides until crispy. Chop and set aside.
5. Place one slice of bread at the bottom of the pie iron. Top with the eggs, bacon, and other ingredients.
6. Place another slice of bread on top.
7. Close and latch the pie iron.
8. Place the pie iron over the coals and cook on both sides until the bread is evenly brown. Check every two minutes.
9. Remove the pie iron from the coals. Serve warm.

Nutrition Facts per Serving
Calories 617, total fat 38.4 g, carb 33.3 g,
Protein 36 g, sodium 1392 mg

Cheddar Hash Brown

There is nothing wrong with a regular hash brown breakfast, but it's just so good to give this classic hash brown recipe a decadent upgrade with avocado and cheddar for an ooey, gooey makeover.

Serves 2 - Prep. time 8–10 minutes
Cooking time 5–10 minutes

Ingredients
½ avocado, roughly chopped and seeded
1 tomato, thinly sliced
2 cups hash brown potatoes
¼ cup shredded cheddar
Salt and pepper to taste
Pinch cayenne (optional)

Directions
1. Prepare the campfire.
2. Grease both sides of the pie iron with butter, vegetable oil, or cooking spray.
3. Add the hash browns on both sides.
4. Add the cheese on both sides.
5. Add the tomato and avocado on both sides. Top with seasoning.
6. Close and latch the pie iron.
7. Place the pie iron over the coals and cook on both sides until the hash browns are golden brown.
8. Remove the pie iron from the coals. Serve warm.

Nutrition Facts per Serving
Calories 546, total fat 30.4 g, carb 60.7 g,
Protein 9.4 g, sodium 625 mg

Blueberry Cheese French Toast

The best thing about this French toast is that it can be eaten as a fruity yet nutritious breakfast as well as a snack and also a light meal. Suit yourself as to whichever time you want to savor this creamy French toast with blueberry goodness.

Serves 2 - Prep. time 5 minutes
Cooking time 5–10 minutes

Ingredients
4 slices bread
1 large egg
2 tablespoons cream cheese
¼ cup blueberries
1 tablespoon milk
½ teaspoon vanilla extract

Directions
1. Prepare the campfire.
2. Smash the cream cheese with the blueberries.
3. Spread the cream cheese mixture over two bread slices.
4. Top with the remaining two bread slices.
5. Beat eggs and mix in the milk and vanilla.
6. Coat the sandwiches with the egg mixture.
7. Grease both sides of the pie iron with butter, vegetable oil, or cooking spray.
8. Add one sandwich. Close and latch the pie iron.
9. Place the pie iron over the coals and cook on both sides until evenly brown.
10. Remove the pie iron from the coals. Repeat with the other sandwich. Serve warm.

Nutrition Facts per Serving
Calories 136, total fat 6.8 g, carb 12.7 g,
Protein 5.7 g, sodium 191 mg

Bacon Egg Breakfast

Add more cheesy and eggy texture to these bacon hash browns by preheating the pie iron before you add any ingredients. This allows the ideal searing of the eggs, hash browns, and bacon.

Serves 4 - Prep. time 5 minutes
Cooking time 8–10 minutes

Ingredients
4 ounces cheddar cheese, shredded
3 cups frozen hash browns, thawed
4 large eggs
4 slices cooked bacon, diced
Salt and pepper to taste
½ cup (1 stick) unsalted butter

Directions
1. Prepare the campfire.
2. Preheat the pie iron.
3. Lightly beat the eggs in a bowl.
4. Add the hash browns, bacon, cheddar, and salt and pepper. Mix well.
5. Add 2 tablespoons of butter to the pie iron and swirl it around to coat both sides.
6. Add ¼ of the potato mixture. Close and latch the pie iron.
7. Place the pie iron over the coals and cook for about 2 minutes, rotating halfway through.
8. Remove the pie iron from the coals. Set the potatoes aside.
9. Repeat with the remaining mixture and serve warm.

Nutrition Facts per Serving
Calories 802, total fat 60 g, carb 42.1 g,
Protein 24.1 g, sodium 1249 mg

Banana French Toast

This banana-stuffed breakfast French toast is popularly known as "Mountain Pie." It is a restaurant standard breakfast that you don't expect to enjoy on a camping trip. A must-try for your next campfire adventure.

Serves 1 - Prep. time 5 minutes
Cooking time 5–10 minutes

Ingredients
1 egg
2–3 tablespoons milk
2 slices bread or cinnamon swirl
2 slices cream cheese
1 teaspoon chopped walnuts
½ banana, sliced
Maple syrup (optional)

Directions
1. Prepare the campfire.
2. Preheat the pie iron and grease both sides with butter, vegetable oil, or cooking spray.
3. Lightly beat the eggs in a bowl. Mix in the milk.
4. Coat the bread slices with the egg mixture.
5. Place one slice of bread over the pie iron and add two cream cheese slice on top.
6. Add the banana and walnuts. Place the other bread slice on top. Close and latch the pie iron.
7. Place the pie iron over the coals and cook on both sides until the bread is evenly brown.
8. Remove the pie iron from the coals. Serve warm with some maple syrup on top.

Nutrition Facts per Serving
Calories 459, total fat 17.7 g, carb 66.7 g,
Protein 11.7 g, sodium 302 mg

Honey Banana Sandwich

A highly recommended breakfast recipe for peanut butter fans. It combines mineral-rich banana along with honey to provide a great balance of taste and nutrition for the perfect start of your camping day.

Serves 1 - Prep. time 5 minutes
Cooking time 8 minutes

Ingredients
2 slices bread
1 banana
2 tablespoons peanut butter
1 tablespoon honey
1 tablespoon cinnamon

Directions
1. Prepare the campfire.
2. Preheat the pie iron and grease both sides with butter.
3. Place one slice of bread at the bottom of the pie iron. Spread peanut butter on top.
4. Add the cinnamon, honey, and banana on top.
5. Place the other slice of bread on top.
6. Close and latch the pie iron.
7. Place the pie iron over the coals and cook on both sides until golden and crispy.
8. Remove the pie iron from the coals. Serve warm with your choice of sliced fruits and a glass of milk.

Nutrition Facts per Serving
Calories 422, total fat 17.2 g, carb 65.1 g,
Protein 11 g, sodium 272 mg

Creamy Bacon Hash Browns

Yet another version of all-time favorite hash browns with a creamy twist of sour cream. Your morning gathering at the campfire with friends and family deserves something special, and these delicious stuffed hash browns are your ideal companion to a steaming cup of hot coffee.

Serves 5–6 - Prep. time 8–10 minutes
Cooking time 10 minutes

Ingredients
1 cup sour cream
1 pound frozen hash browns, thawed
1 green onion, thinly sliced
4 strips bacon, cooked and crumbled
½ cup cheddar cheese, shredded

Directions
1. Prepare the campfire.
2. Grease both sides of the pie iron with butter, vegetable oil, or cooking spray.
3. Add half of the hash browns to create a thin layer.
4. Combine the bacon, green onion, and sour cream in a bowl.
5. Add the sour cream mixture on top of the hash browns; spread evenly.
6. Add cheese and then create another hash brown layer on top. Close and latch the pie iron.
7. Place the pie iron over the coals and cook on both sides for 2–3 minutes total until the hash browns are evenly browned and cooked well.
8. Remove the pie iron from the coals. Serve warm.

Nutrition Facts per Serving
Calories 390, total fat 25.9 g, carb 28.7 g,
Protein 10.6 g, sodium 630 mg

SANDWICHES AND BREAD

Ham and Cheese Sandwich

What's not to adore about this classic cheesy ham sandwich? It has variety, taste, and more importantly, convenience as it's ready in just a few minutes. Everything tastes better at the campfire, but this sandwich beats your expectations. Start stuffing these ingredients into your camping bag and make this as your first meal on the first camping day.

Serves 1 - Prep. time 5 minutes
Cooking time 5–10 minutes

Ingredients
1 avocado, seeded and sliced
2 tablespoon mayonnaise
2 tablespoon honey mustard
1 teaspoon original cayenne pepper sauce Frank's Red Hot
2–3 slices cheese (provolone, cheddar, or Swiss)
1 slice cooked deli pre-sliced meat (turkey, ham, roast beef, etc.)

Directions
1. Prepare the campfire.
2. Grease both sides of the pie iron with butter, vegetable oil, or cooking spray.
3. Place one slice of bread at the bottom of the pie iron. Add the mustard and Frank's Red Hot sauce.
4. Add a cheese slice and some sliced deli meat. Add the avocado slices on top.
5. Add 1–2 additional cheese slices and the mayonnaise. Place the other bread on top.
6. Close and latch the pie iron.
7. Place the pie iron over the coals and cook on both sides until golden brown.
8. Remove the pie iron from the coals. Serve warm.

23

Nutrition Facts per Serving
Calories 1194, total fat 102.4 g, carb 35.8 g,
Protein 36.7 g, sodium 1402 mg

Cheesesteak Sandwich

These veggies and steak stuffed sandwiches are absolutely delicious and full of hearty flavors. If you love steak, you will definitely love this cheesesteak sandwich. This is a simple, hardy, and filling sandwich for everyone.

Serves 5 - Prep. time 10 minutes
Cooking time 40 minutes

Ingredients
Green and red bell pepper, sliced
1 pound sirloin steak, cut into strips
1 tablespoon olive oil
1 yellow onion, sliced
Salt and pepper to taste
3½ ounces provolone cheese, sliced
¼ cup butter, softened
10 slices bread

Directions
1. Prepare the campfire.
2. Add the steak, peppers, yellow onion, olive oil, salt, and pepper to a tinfoil pocket. Shake well.
3. Cook over the coals for 30 minutes.
4. Spread butter over two bread slices.
5. Place one slice of bread in the pie iron. Add ⅓ cup of the steak mixture.
6. Place a cheese slice on top.
7. Close and latch the pie iron.
8. Place the pie iron over the coals and cook for about 10 minutes total, rotating after 5 minutes, until evenly brown.
9. Remove the pie iron from the coals. Repeat with the other sandwiches. Serve warm.

Nutrition Facts per Serving
Calories 649, total fat 41.7 g, carb 15.3 g,
Protein 52.1 g, sodium 1020 mg

Spaghetti Sandwich

If you think that spaghetti is only for indoor cooking, think again. Yes, you don't have to miss out on spaghetti at your campfire. If you are late setting up, this recipe is perfect for the first night of camping. Enjoy the beauty of nature and freedom in the company of this scrumptious Italian seasoned sandwich.

Serves 1 - Prep. time 10 minutes
Cooking time 6–8 minutes

Ingredients
1 cup spaghetti sauce, ready-to-serve
½ cup spaghetti pasta (about ½ cup per sandwich)
2 slices bread per sandwich
¾ cup butter
2 teaspoons Italian seasoning
2 teaspoons garlic powder or crushed garlic

Directions
1. Prepare the campfire.
2. Cook the spaghetti in a skillet filled with salted water; drain and set aside. (You can also pre-cook it at home.)
3. Combine the spaghetti and spaghetti sauce in a bowl. Set aside for 5–10 minutes.
4. In another bowl, combine the garlic, butter, and Italian seasoning.
5. Grease both sides of the pie iron with cooking spray.
6. Spread garlic butter over a slice of bread and place it butter side down at the bottom of the pie iron.
7. Add ½ cup of spaghetti and top with another garlic-buttered bread slice.
8. Close and latch the pie iron.
9. Place the pie iron over the coals and cook for 6–8 minutes, flipping every 1–2 minutes.
10. Remove the pie iron from the coals. Serve warm.

Nutrition Facts per Serving
Calories 1944, total fat 152 g, carb 126.8 g,
Protein 23.2 g, sodium 2432 mg

Lobster Roll Sandwich

If you can't get your hands-on lobster meat, you can substitute it with imitation crab meat. However, real lobster chunks make this sandwich so incredibly tasty you'll crave it more and more. Mayonnaise and hot sauce add an additional flavor punch to this great-tasting sandwich.

Serves 4 - Prep. time 8–10 minutes
Cooking time 10–15 minutes

Ingredients
Mayonnaise to taste
Lemon juice to taste
Hot sauce to taste
Salt and pepper to taste
½ cup butter or 1 stick
½ cup lobster chunks per sandwich
2 slices of white bread or English Muffin Toasting Bread

Directions
1. Prepare the campfire.
2. Melt at least 1 stick of butter in a skillet; this is sufficient to make 4 sandwiches.
3. Remove from heat and add the lobster. Mix in the lemon juice and one or two dashes of hot sauce. Toss well.
4. Place one slice of bread at the bottom of the pie iron. Spread mayonnaise and add lobster meat on top.
5. Spread mayonnaise over another bread slice and place it on top. Close and latch the pie iron.
6. Place the pie iron over the coals and cook on both sides until golden brown.
7. Remove the pie iron from the coals. Serve warm.

Nutrition Facts per Serving
Calories 267, total fat 24.8 g, carb 9.8 g,
Protein 2.3 g, sodium 350 mg

Baked Beans Brown Bread Sandwich

Haven't heard about bean sandwiches before? Then you're in for a real camping surprise! You can't go wrong with this basic yet delicious baked bean sandwich. It's time to gather around and make this camping friendly sandwich to make the most of your wilderness adventure trip.

Serves 1 - Prep. time 10 minutes
Cooking time 10–15 minutes

Ingredients
1 can brown bread (optionally with raisins)
2 strips bacon for each sandwich
1 can baked beans
Finely chopped onion (optional)

Directions
1. Prepare the campfire.
2. Add the bacon to a skillet and cook on both sides until crispy. Drain over paper towels and set aside.
3. Slice the brown bread into ½-inch-thick slices.
4. Grease both sides of the pie iron with butter, vegetable oil, or cooking spray.
5. Place one slice of bread at the bottom of the pie iron. Add two strips of bacon, crumbling them as needed.
6. Add a large spoonful of beans and chopped onion.
7. Place another slice of bread on top.
8. Close and latch the pie iron.
9. Place the pie iron over the coals and cook on both sides until golden brown.
10. Remove the pie iron from the coals. Serve warm.

Nutrition Facts per Serving
Calories 1294, total fat 34.1 g, carb 212 g,
Protein 47 g, sodium 4093 mg

Egg Sausage Sandwich

Unlike any other egg-based sandwich, this one includes a separately fried egg to create a unique texture for an ultimate meal experience. Either bacon or sausage patty pairs wonderfully with the separately fried egg and biscuit dough. It's simple and awesome.

Serves 1 - Prep. time 5 minutes
Cooking time 10 minutes

Ingredients
1 slice cheddar cheese
Dough of 1 biscuit
1 sausage patty or two strips of bacon (optional)
1 egg

Directions
1. Prepare the campfire.
2. Preheat the pie iron and grease both sides with butter, vegetable oil, or cooking spray.
3. Place the dough at the bottom of the pie iron.
4. Close and latch the pie iron.
5. Place the pie iron over the coals and cook for about 2 minutes. Flip and cook for 2 more minutes until brown on top.
6. Add the bacon or sausage to a skillet and cook on both sides until crispy and evenly brown.
7. Slice the cooked dough, add the sausage and cheese, and set aside.
8. Open the pie iron, crack the egg into it, and without closing, cook over the coals until the egg white starts to set.
9. Close the pie iron, flip it, and cook until the egg is cooked to your satisfaction.
10. Top the biscuit with the cooked egg and serve warm.

Nutrition Facts per Serving
Calories 653, total fat 49.1 g, carb 26.7 g,
Protein 25.3 g, sodium 1316 mg

Garlic Bread

Only the thought of having garlic bread on an adventurous camping trip is enough to bring a big smile. This absolutely mouthwatering bread needs only a few basic ingredients, and it is ridiculously easy and quick to prepare.

Serves 4 - Prep. time 5 minutes
Cooking time 10–12 minutes

Ingredients
1 teaspoon garlic powder
½ teaspoon parsley
¼ cup butter, softened
2 roll of Crescent Rolls Big N Flaky Pillsbury

Directions
1. Prepare the campfire.
2. Grease both sides of the pie iron with butter, vegetable oil, or cooking spray.
3. Combine the parsley, garlic powder, and butter in a bowl.
4. Place one roll at the bottom of the pie iron and spread with 1 teaspoon of garlic butter. Add another roll on top and spread with some more garlic butter.
5. Add another roll-on top.
6. Close and latch the pie iron.
7. Place the pie iron over the coals and cook for about 6 minutes. Flip and cook for 6 more minutes until the dough is evenly golden.
8. Remove the pie iron from the coals. Serve warm.

Nutrition Facts per Serving
Calories 179, total fat 15 g, carb 10 g,
Protein 1.2 g, sodium 247 mg

Turkey Egg Sandwich

If you are looking for an interesting camping recipe that combines turkey, ham, and cheese, then this hearty sandwich will absolutely do it. Also known as a Monte Cristo sandwich, for lunch, it can't get easier than this.

Serves 1 - Prep. time 5 minutes
Cooking time 5–10 minutes

Ingredients
2 slices turkey
2 slices ham
2 slices cheddar cheese
1 egg
2 slices bread
1 tablespoon milk
Powdered sugar to taste

Directions
1. Prepare the campfire.
2. Grease both sides of the pie iron with butter, vegetable oil, or cooking spray.
3. Lightly beat the eggs in a bowl. Mix in the milk.
4. Evenly coat the bread with the egg mixture.
5. Place one slice of bread at the bottom of the pie iron. Add the ham, turkey, and cheese on top.
6. Place the other slice of bread on top.
7. Close and latch the pie iron.
8. Place the pie iron over the coals and cook for about 5 minutes. Flip and cook for 5 more minutes.
9. Remove the pie iron from the coals. Serve warm with powdered sugar on top.

Nutrition Facts per Serving
Calories 556, total fat 30.1 g, carb 24.7 g,
Protein 45.3 g, sodium 2142 mg

Classic Tomato Cheese Sandwich

Bring alive the classic Caprese flavor of basil, tomato, and mozzarella in this vinegar glazed cheese sandwich. Using balsamic vinegar instead of regular vinegar prevents the bread from getting soggy. This sandwich is perfect to carry around and eat on the go.

Serves 1 - Prep. time 5 minutes
Cooking time 5–10 minutes

Ingredients
1 slice mozzarella
2 slices tomato (you can also use canned tomatoes)
3 basil leaves
2 slices bread
Balsamic vinegar glaze

Directions
1. Prepare the campfire.
2. Grease both sides of the pie iron with butter, vegetable oil, or cooking spray.
3. Place one slice of bread at the bottom of the pie iron. Add the tomato and cheese slices.
4. Add the basil leaves on top. Drizzle with balsamic vinegar glaze.
5. Place the other slice of bread on top. Close and latch the pie iron.
6. Place the pie iron over the coals and cook for about 3 minutes. Flip and cook for 2–3 more minutes until evenly brown.
7. Remove the pie iron from the coals. Serve warm.

Nutrition Facts per Serving
Calories 174, total fat 5.7 g, carb 20.3 g,
Protein 9.7 g, sodium 304 mg

PIZZAS AND PIES

Pepperoni Pizza

Pepperoni pizza is incredibly popular among campfire adventurers. Not only it is quick to prepare, but it's every bit as full of pizza flavor as the ones you get delivered at home. It's time to savor this pizza with a pepperoni flavor twist.

Serves 4 - Prep. time 5 minutes
Cooking time 10 minutes

Ingredients
¾ pound mozzarella cheese, shredded
1 (13½-ounce) package Pillsbury pizza crust dough
1 cup pizza sauce
½ pound pepperoni, sliced

Directions
1. Prepare the campfire.
2. Unroll the pizza dough and cut it into four rectangles.
3. Grease both sides of the pie iron with butter, vegetable oil, or cooking spray.
4. Place half of one dough rectangle at the bottom of the pie iron. Add the toppings.
5. Fold the other half over.
6. Close and latch the pie iron.
7. Place the pie iron over the coals and cook on both sides for 5 minutes total until evenly brown.
8. Remove the pie iron from the coals. Repeat with the other pizzas. Serve warm.

Nutrition Facts per Serving
Calories 894, total fat 46.5 g, carb 91.6 g,
Protein 25.6 g, sodium 2144 mg

Olive Mushroom Pizza

When you offer this exotic campfire pizza to your camping buddies, get ready for a lot of compliments. This succulent olive pizza is filled with cheesy taste; it makes a great campfire dinner.

Serves 10 - Prep. time 5 minutes
Cooking time 8–10 minutes

Ingredients
1 pound mozzarella cheese, shredded
2 cups pizza sauce
⅔ cup Kalamata olives, diced
⅔ cup black olives, diced
½ pound pepperoni, sliced
⅔ cup fresh mushrooms, sliced
Fresh parmesan, grated (optional)
20 slices bread—white, wheat or sourdough

Directions
1. Prepare the campfire.
2. Spread butter over two bread slices and stick them together.
3. Add 1 tablespoon of pizza sauce and spread evenly. Add 2 tablespoons of cheese and 1 tablespoon of each of the toppings.
4. Top with the grated parmesan and some more pizza sauce (optional).
5. Close and latch the pie iron.
6. Place the pie iron over the coals and cook for about 4–5 minutes. Flip and cook for 4–5 more minutes until evenly brown.
7. Remove the pie iron from the coals. Serve warm.

Nutrition Facts per Serving
Calories 393, total fat 18.7 g, carb 37.6 g,
Protein 18.8 g, sodium 1280 mg

Pineapple Ham Pizza Pockets

After we tried out this pineapple pizza on our last camping trip, it has become our favorite. We will never miss packing these ingredients when we are planning a camping trip. And yes, you can experiment by adding your choice of toppings to customize it to your taste preferences.

Serves 4 - Prep. time 8–10 minutes
Cooking time 1 minute

Ingredients
4 ham slices
1 cup pizza sauce
1 can crushed pineapple
Grated cheese and other toppings of your choice (optional)
8 slices bread

Directions
1. Prepare the campfire.
2. Grease both sides of the pie iron with some butter.
3. Place one slice of bread at the bottom of the pie iron. Add the pizza sauce and toppings. You can add more pizza sauce on top if you want.
4. Place another slice of bread on top.
5. Close and latch the pie iron.
6. Place the pie iron over the coals and cook on both sides for 6–8 minutes total until golden brown.
7. Remove the pie iron from the coals. Repeat for remaining bread.
8. Serve warm.

Nutrition Facts per Serving
Calories 142, total fat 4.6 g, carb 16.4 g,
Protein 8.5 g, sodium 613 mg

Pepperoni Tortilla Pizza Pockets

Filling tortillas, perky pepperoni, and mouthwatering mozzarella get together in these delicious pizza pockets to make the ultimate campfire meal.

Serves 4 - Prep. time 5 minutes
Cooking time 10 minutes

Ingredients
⅜ cup pizza sauce
½ pound pepperoni, sliced
1 cup mozzarella cheese, shredded
4 10-inch tortillas

Directions
1. Prepare the campfire.
2. Grease both sides of the pie iron with butter, vegetable oil, or cooking spray.
3. Place half of one tortilla at the bottom of the pie iron. Add the pizza sauce and toppings.
4. Fold over the other tortilla half to create a pocket. Close and latch the pie iron.
5. Place the pie iron over the coals and cook for about 3–5 minutes. Flip and cook for 3–5 more minutes until evenly cooked.
6. Remove the pie iron from the coals. Serve.

Nutrition Facts per Serving
Calories 434, total fat 28 g, carb 27.5 g,
Protein 18.4 g, sodium 1018 mg

Coney Dog Pie

This pie is a great way to utilize leftover meat. The Coney dog pie with generously buttered bread is a filling meal that keeps you full for hours. This pie is easy, frugal, and simply delicious.

Serves 1 - Prep. time 5 minutes
Cooking time 5–10 minutes

Ingredients
1 hot dog, halved
Leftover taco meat
1 Cheddar cheese, sliced or shredded
1 tablespoon butter
2 white bread slices or bucket dough

Directions
1. Prepare the campfire.
2. Generously grease both sides of the pie iron with butter.
3. Place one slice of bread or dough at the bottom of the pie iron. Add 2–3 tablespoons of taco meat.
4. Add half of a hot dog. Add ½ cheese slice or ½ shredded cheese slice.
5. Place another slice of bread or dough on top.
6. Close and latch the pie iron.
7. Place the pie iron over the coals and cook on both sides until evenly brown.
8. Remove the pie iron from the coals. Serve warm.

Nutrition Facts per Serving
Calories 533, total fat 36.1 g, carb 27.7 g,
Protein 10.6 g, sodium 1267 mg

Cream Cheese Pie

In mere minutes, this creamy pie is ready to blow your mind with its cheesy texture and flavors. This simple and easy pie never fails to win hearts.

Serves 4 - Prep. time 5 minutes
Cooking time 5–10 minutes

Ingredients
4 tablespoons cream cheese
1 (8-ounce) container crescent rolls
Powdered sugar
1 can (21 ounces) cherry pie filling

Directions
1. Prepare the campfire.
2. Grease both sides of the pie iron with butter, vegetable oil, or cooking spray.
3. Roll out the crescent rolls into two triangles. Press them together, especially at the seams.
4. Press dough into a 9-inch-long piece. Divide into halves.
5. Place one half at the bottom of the pie iron. Add 2 tablespoons of cherry pie filling and 1 tablespoon of cream cheese.
6. Place the other half on top. Seal the edges by gently pressing down.
7. Close and latch the pie iron.
8. Place the pie iron over the coals and cook on both sides for 5–8 minutes until evenly golden.
9. Remove the pie iron from the coals. Serve warm sprinkled with powdered sugar.

Nutrition Facts per Serving
Calories 397, total fat 7.3 g, carb 75.4g,
Protein 7.5 g, sodium 360 mg

Chicken Pot Pie

Filled with smartly chosen ingredients, this chicken pot pie has a high satiety factor, just like peanuts and bananas. The magic of this homely comfort food can easily be recreated at the campsite. After a long, tiring day of hiking, this pot pie is your go-to warm meal.

Serves 1 - Prep. time 8–10 minutes
Cooking time 5 minutes

Ingredients

1 can mixed vegetables, drained
6 ounces grilled chicken breast strips
1 can cream of chicken
1 teaspoon chicken bouillon granules
2 tubes Pillsbury big crescent rolls
Salt and pepper to taste

Directions

1. Prepare the campfire.
2. Add the chicken strips, vegetables, cream of chicken, chicken bouillon, salt, and pepper to a plastic bag or container. Shake well to combine.
3. Grease both sides of the pie iron with butter, vegetable oil, or cooking spray.
4. Roll the crescent rolls into triangles.
5. Place one roll at the bottom of the pie iron. Add ⅓–½ cup of the chicken mixture on top.
6. Place another roll on top. Press down the edges.
7. Close and latch the pie iron.
8. Place the pie iron over the coals and cook for about 2 minutes. Flip and cook for 2 more minutes until evenly cooked.
9. Remove the pie iron from the coals. Serve warm.

Nutrition Facts per Serving
Calories 883, total fat 38.2 g, carb 79.5 g,
Protein 52.9 g, sodium 4776 mg

Apple Potato Bread Pie

We all have made apple pie at home, but this is another fancy way of enjoying this popular pie recipe at the campsite. This pie is full of delectable and tongue-tingling flavors.

Serves 6 - Prep. time 10 minutes
Cooking time 8 minutes

Ingredients
12 slices potato bread
Juice and zest of 1 lemon
4 large apples (all red, or mixed green and red), thinly sliced
½ cup sugar
½ cup brown sugar
1¼ teaspoons cinnamon
Pinch cayenne pepper
½ cup (1 stick) unsalted butter
2 (1-gallon) Ziploc bags
Whipped Cream
2 tablespoons powdered sugar
1 cup whipping cream
1 teaspoon vanilla

Directions
1. Prepare the campfire.
2. Combine the whipping cream, powdered sugar, and vanilla in a bowl.
3. Add the apple slices and lemon zest and juice to a Ziploc bag. Shake to combine well.
4. Add the cinnamon, sugar, and nutmeg to the other Ziploc bag. Shake to combine well.
5. Combine the contents of both Ziploc bags and set aside.
6. Grease both sides of the pie iron with butter, vegetable oil, or cooking spray.

7. Place one slice of bread at the bottom of the pie iron. Spread some butter on top. Add one-sixth of the apple mixture on top.
8. Place another slice of bread on top.
9. Close and latch the pie iron.
10. Place the pie iron over the coals and cook for about 4 minutes. Flip and cook for 4 more minutes until evenly browned.
11. Remove the pie iron from the coals. Serve warm with a whipped cream mixture on top.

Nutrition Facts per Serving

Calories 557, total fat 23.9 g, carb 85.4 g,
Protein 7.1 g, sodium 462 mg

CAMPING MEALS

Bean Cheddar Quesadillas

After a long, tiring day of outdoor camping, we all crave a decent, hearty meal that is quick to cook and full of delicious goodness. These bean quesadillas make a great, satisfying meal that will keep you full for hours.

Serves 6 - Prep. time 5 minutes
Cooking time 5–10 minutes

Ingredients
12 flour or corn tortillas
1 (16-ounce) can refried beans
¾ pound shredded sharp cheddar
Salsa to taste

Directions
1. Prepare the campfire.
2. Grease both sides of the pie iron with butter, vegetable oil, or cooking spray.
3. Place half of a corn tortilla at the bottom of the pie iron. Add refried beans and cheese.
4. Fold the other half of the tortilla over.
5. Close and latch the pie iron.
6. Place the pie iron over the coals and cook on both sides until the tortilla is evenly toasted.
7. Remove the pie iron from the coals. Serve warm with salsa on top.

Nutrition Facts per Serving
Calories 1411, total fat 60.1 g, carb 122.6 g,
Protein 95.1 g, sodium 2213 mg

Cheese Tater Tots

One great thing about these tater tots is that you can play with the recipe by creating different versions with your favorite toppings and cheese varieties. The fun has no limit!

Serves 2 - Prep. time 5 minutes
Cooking time 5–6 minutes

Ingredients
Tater tots, thawed
1 green bell pepper, minced
1 onion, minced
1 garlic salt, salt and pepper to taste
1 cup cheddar cheese, shredded

Directions
1. Prepare the campfire.
2. Grease both sides of the pie iron with butter, vegetable oil, or cooking spray.
3. Place one layer of tater tots at the bottom of the pie iron. Season with garlic salt, salt, and pepper to taste.
4. Add green bell pepper and onion.
5. Place another slice of bread on top.
6. Close and latch the pie iron.
7. Place the pie iron over the coals and cook for about 4–5 minutes. Flip and cook for 4–5 minutes more.
8. An open pie iron, add the cheese and cook for 1 minute more.
9. Remove the pie iron from the coals. Serve warm.

Nutrition Facts per Serving
Calories 301, total fat 20.6 g, carb 14.6 g,
Protein 15.8 g, sodium 360 mg

Sirloin Steak Fajitas

If you plan to keep yourself warm and full for hours, these fajitas are your go-to camping meal. Just make them whenever the mood strikes and we promise you that you won't be sorry.

Serves 4 - Prep. time 5 minutes
Cooking time 10 minutes

Ingredients
1 yellow bell pepper, sliced
1 orange bell pepper, sliced
1 green bell pepper, sliced
1 medium yellow onion, sliced
1 pound sirloin steak, cut into strips
2 tablespoons taco seasoning
1 tablespoon olive oil
½ cup salsa (optional)
½ cup sour cream (optional)
1 cup Tex-Mex cheese
4 (10-inch) tortillas

Directions
1. Prepare the campfire.
2. Add the steak, peppers, onions, olive oil and taco seasoning to a tinfoil packet. Shake to combine.
3. Cook over coals for 25–30 minutes.
4. Grease both sides of the pie iron with butter, vegetable oil, or cooking spray.
5. Place half of a corn tortilla at the bottom of the pie iron. Add fajita steak mixture and cheese over.
6. Fold the other half of the tortilla over.
7. Close and latch the pie iron.
8. Place the pie iron over the coals and cook on both sides for 5–10 minutes until the tortilla is evenly toasted.
9. Remove the pie iron from the coals. Serve warm with salsa and sour cream on top.

Nutrition Facts per Serving
Calories 515, total fat 23.1 g, carb 29.8 g,
Protein 46.1 g, sodium 1269 mg

Beef Tacos

These tacos might need a bit of effort to prepare, but there's nothing more comforting and filling. Get in touch with your inner pioneer and start packing ingredients for this hearty recipe.

Serves 6 - Prep. time 8–10 minutes
Cooking time 20 minutes

Ingredients
1 (1-ounce) package taco seasoning mix
1 pound ground beef
1 cup shredded Monterey Jack cheese
1 can chopped tomatoes
12 (5-inch) corn tortillas
1 cup sour cream
1 cup salsa
2 cups shredded iceberg lettuce (optional)
½ cup chopped onion (optional)

Directions
1. Prepare the campfire.
2. Add the ground beef to a skillet and cook over the coals until evenly browned.
3. Remove excess fat and mix in the taco seasoning.
4. Grease both sides of the pie iron with butter, vegetable oil, or cooking spray.
5. Place a tortilla at the bottom of the pie iron. Scoop some of the ground beef over it.
6. Add some cheese and onion on top.
7. Top with another tortilla.
8. Close and latch the pie iron.
9. Place the pie iron over the coals and cook on both sides until the tortilla is browned and crisped.
10. Remove the pie iron from the coals. Serve warm with lettuce, salsa, sour cream, and tomatoes.

Nutrition Facts per Serving
Calories 444, total fat 20.3 g, carb 32.5 g,
Protein 32.5 g, sodium 919 mg

Avocado Toast

If you think that you need to visit a fancy restaurant to have avocado toast, you are in for a big surprise. This wonderful avocado toast you can easily make at a campfire with just a few easy-to-source ingredients.

Serves 2 - Prep. time 8–10 minutes
Cooking time 10 minutes

Ingredients
1 clove garlic, crushed (optional)
1 avocado, seeded and halved
Juice of 1 lemon
Salt and pepper to taste
4 (4-inch) tortillas
½ tablespoon olive oil

Directions
1. Prepare the campfire.
2. Scoop out the avocado flesh and mash or crush it in a bowl.
3. Add the garlic, lemon juice, olive oil, salt, and pepper; mix well.
4. Grease both sides of the pie iron with butter, vegetable oil, or cooking spray.
5. Place one tortilla at the bottom of the pie iron. Add half of the avocado mixture.
6. Place another tortilla on top.
7. Close and latch the pie iron.
8. Place the pie iron over the coals and cook on both sides until evenly cooked.
9. Remove the pie iron from the coals. Repeat the process with the other tortillas. Serve warm.

Nutrition Facts per Serving

Calories 348, total fat 24.7 g, carb 31.1 g,
Protein 5 g, sodium 33 mg

Chicken Chimichangas

These chicken chimichangas are the perfect way to impress your campfire buddies with minimal effort. This is an all-in-one healthy, tasty, and filling meal to have with your camping friends.

Serves 4 - Prep. time 5 minutes
Cooking time 8–10 minutes

Ingredients
½ cup onion, chopped
½ cup green pepper, chopped
1 cup chicken, cut into bite-sized pieces
¼ teaspoon ground cumin
Garlic salt, salt and pepper to taste
¼ cup picante or enchilada sauce, green or red
½ cup cheddar cheese, cubed
4 (7-inch) flour tortillas

Directions
1. Prepare the campfire.
2. Add some cooking oil to a skillet.
3. Add the chicken, onion, and green pepper; stir-cook until the chicken is evenly browned.
4. Add the cumin, garlic salt, salt, and pepper; cook for a few minutes until fragrant.
5. Add the enchilada sauce and remove from heat. Add the cheese and mix until it melts.
6. Grease both sides of the pie iron with butter, vegetable oil, or cooking spray.
7. Place half of one tortilla at the bottom of the pie iron. Add ¼ of the chicken mixture.
8. Flip the other half of the tortilla on top and press the edges together to create a rectangular pocket.
9. Close and latch the pie iron.
10. Place the pie iron over the coals and cook on both sides until evenly brown.

11. Remove the pie iron from the coals. Serve warm with your choice of toppings (sour cream, lettuce, tomato, salsa, refried beans, etc.).

Nutrition Facts per Serving
Calories 177, total fat 6.6 g, carb 14.5 g,
Protein 15.6 g, sodium 123 mg

Ham Crescents

If you can't go without meat-based meals on a camping trip, be sure to pack these ingredients.

Serves 1 - Prep. Time 5 minutes
Cooking time 10 minutes

Ingredients
1 slice of cheddar cheese
1 slice of ham
2 Pillsbury crescent rolls or sliced bread

Directions
1. Prepare the campfire.
2. Grease both sides of the pie iron with butter, vegetable oil, or cooking spray.
3. Place one roll or bread slice at the bottom of the pie iron. Add 1 ham piece and 1 cheese slice.
4. Place another roll or bread slice on top.
5. Close and latch the pie iron.
6. Place the pie iron over the coals and cook for about 4–5 minutes. Flip and cook for 4–5 more minutes.
7. Remove the pie iron from the coals. Serve warm.

Nutrition Facts per Serving
Calories 358, total fat 23.7 g, carb 23.4 g,
Protein 13.6 g, sodium 979 mg

Chicken Tortilla Wrap

This tortilla wrap is a gourmet, filling, and healthy recipe that needs no introduction.

Serves 1 - Prep. time 5 minutes
Cooking time 5 minutes

Ingredients
1 tablespoon pesto
2–3 slices cooked chicken breast
2 tablespoons mozzarella cheese, shredded
1 tortilla

Directions
1. Prepare the campfire.
2. Grease both sides of the pie iron with butter, vegetable oil, or cooking spray.
3. Place half of the tortilla at the bottom of the pie iron. Add the chicken, pesto, and cheese.
4. Fold the other half of the tortilla over to make a pocket. Close and latch the pie iron.
5. Place the pie iron over the coals and cook for about 3 minutes. Flip and cook for 3 more minutes.
6. Remove the pie iron from the coals. Serve warm.

Nutrition Facts per Serving
Calories 330, total fat 17.4 g, carb 15.1 g,
Protein 29.5 g, sodium 1131 mg

Chicken Tomato Croissant

This chicken croissant is a terrific twist on the old style of croissant.

Serves 1 - Prep. time 5 minutes
Cooking time 10 minutes

Ingredients
3 sun-dried tomatoes
¼ cup goat cheese, crumbled
2 Pillsbury crescent rolls
1 Roasted chicken breast, sliced

Directions
1. Prepare the campfire.
2. Grease both sides of the pie iron with butter, vegetable oil, or cooking spray.
3. Place one roll at the bottom of the pie iron. Add the chicken, goat cheese, and tomatoes.
4. Place another roll on top.
5. Close and latch the pie iron.
6. Place the pie iron over the coals and cook for about 4–5 minutes. Flip and cook for 4–5 more minutes.
7. Remove the pie iron from the coals. Serve warm.

Nutrition Facts per Serving
Calories 269, total fat 14.1 g, carb 26.5 g,
Protein 11.2 g, sodium 1056 mg

DESSERTS AND COOKIES

Strawberry Shortcake

One thing is for sure when you pass this shortcake around—it won't last long. The juicy and incredibly delightful strawberries along with the goodness of honey make this shortcake simply irresistible.

Serves 8 - Prep. time 5 minutes
Cooking time 10 minutes

Ingredients
½ cup honey
1 can biscuit dough
½ cup cream cheese, softened
1 cup strawberries, sliced

Directions
1. Prepare the campfire.
2. Grease both sides of the pie iron with butter, vegetable oil, or cooking spray.
3. Cut the biscuit dough in half.
4. Place one half at the bottom of the pie iron. Spread with 1 tablespoon of cream cheese.
5. Add 1 tablespoon of honey and sliced strawberries.
6. Place the other dough half on top and press the edges together to seal.
7. Close and latch the pie iron.
8. Place the pie iron over the coals and cook for about 2 minutes. Flip and cook for 2 minutes more.
9. Remove the pie iron from the coals. Serve warm.

Nutrition Facts per Serving
Calories 541, total fat 25.1 g, carb 71.2 g,
Protein 11.3 g, sodium 1344 mg

Camp Cookies

We all love how cookies fill up the void in our everyday food routine. Cookies are not just for home, as you can easily prepare them using a pie iron in just a few minutes.

Yield 8 cookies - Prep. time 5 minutes
Cooking time 10–12 minutes

Ingredients
Sugar Cookie Dough Pillsbury

Directions
1. Prepare the campfire.
2. Grease both sides of the pie iron with butter, vegetable oil, or cooking spray.
3. Add 2 tablespoon of cookie dough to the bottom of the pie iron. Press down gently. Repeat on the other side of the pie iron.
4. Without closing it, place the pie iron over the coals and cook for about 12 minutes until the cookies are slightly golden on the edges.
5. Remove the pie iron from the coals. Repeat with the remaining dough. Serve warm.

Nutrition Facts per Serving
Calories 170, total fat 9 g, carb 22 g,
Protein 2 g, sodium 100 mg

Cinnamon Buns

Cinnamon buns are stapled desserts for campfire lovers. They are aromatic, sweet, and look simply gorgeous for the perfect post-meal sweet satisfaction.

Yield 5 buns - Prep. time 5 minutes
Cooking time 15 minutes

Ingredients
10 Pillsbury cinnamon rolls
Frosting of your choice

Directions
1. Prepare the campfire.
2. Grease both sides of the pie iron with butter, vegetable oil, or cooking spray.
3. Place one roll at the bottom of the pie iron.
4. Place another roll on top.
5. Close and latch the pie iron.
6. Place the pie iron over the coals and cook on both sides for about 15 minutes total.
7. Remove the pie iron from the coals. Serve warm with your choice of frosting on top.

Nutrition Facts per Serving
Calories 47, total fat 1.3 g, carb 8.5 g,
Protein 0.5 g, sodium 50 mg

Lemon or Chocolate Dessert Pie

This lemon/chocolate pie is your sweetest excuse to fulfill the demands of your sweet tooth. The combination of marshmallows and lemon curd is too deliciously gorgeous to miss out on. You can make another version of the same pie with chocolate balls and caramel spread.

Serves 1 - Prep. time 10 minutes
Cooking time 5–10 minutes

Ingredients
2 slices white bread
Lemon Meringue Pie
4 white marshmallows
1 tablespoon Lemon curd
Chocolate Caramel Pie
Lindt milk chocolate balls, halved
2 tablespoons caramel spread

Directions
1. Prepare the campfire.
2. Grease both sides of the pie iron with butter, vegetable oil, or cooking spray.
3. Place one slice of bread at the bottom of the pie iron. Add the lemon pie or chocolate pie ingredients one by one.
4. Place another slice of bread on top. Cut off the edges.
5. Close and latch the pie iron.
6. Place the pie iron over the coals and cook on both sides until evenly golden brown.
7. Remove the pie iron from the coals. Serve warm.

Nutrition Facts per Serving
Calories 610, total fat 23.6 g, carb 100.1 g,
Protein 5.6 g, sodium 506 mg

Apple Marshmallow Pie

Gather around the campfire on a calm evening to savor this delish apple marshmallow pie and get lost in its marvelous pie flavors.

Serves 1 - Prep. time 5 minutes
Cooking time 10 minutes

Ingredients
1 can (21 ounces) apple pie filling
1 bag marshmallows
2 biscuits Biscuits Country Pillsbury

Directions
1. Prepare the campfire.
2. Grease both sides of the pie iron with butter, vegetable oil, or cooking spray.
3. Place one biscuit at the bottom of the pie iron. Add ¼ cup of apple pie filling and marshmallows to taste.
4. Place another biscuit on top.
5. Close and latch the pie iron.
6. Place the pie iron over the coals and cook for about 5–6 minutes. Flip and cook for 5–6 more minutes until evenly browned.
7. Remove the pie iron from the coals. Serve.

Nutrition Facts per Serving
Calories 985, total fat 4.6 g, carb 235.3 g,
Protein 9.6 g, sodium 1440 mg

Banana Nutella Biscuits

Presenting dessert biscuits made tempting with mouthwatering Nutella spread and sliced bananas.

Serves 1 - Prep. time 5 minutes
Cooking time 10 minutes

Ingredients
1 banana, sliced into rounds
2 tablespoon Nutella spread
Pillsbury biscuit dough

Directions
1. Prepare the campfire.
2. Grease both sides of the pie iron with butter, vegetable oil, or cooking spray.
3. Place one biscuit at the bottom of the pie iron. Spread with Nutella and add banana rounds on top.
4. Place another biscuit on top.
5. Close and latch the pie iron.
6. Place the pie iron over the coals and cook for 4–5 minutes on each side.
7. Remove the pie iron from the coals. Serve warm.

Nutrition Facts per Serving
Calories 698, total fat 32.6 g, carb 94.9 g,
Protein 9.3 g, sodium 631 mg

Cinnamon Fruit Pie

What could be a more comforting campfire dessert than this recipe that allows you to be creative with your fruit choices? No matter when you are going for a camping trip, just bring along seasonal fruits and make the best fruity pie.

Serves 1 - Prep. time 5 minutes
Cooking time 5 minutes

Ingredients
1 tablespoon cinnamon and sugar mixture
1 can (74 grams) Seasonal fruit (blueberries, raspberries, sweet cherries, apple slices, peach slices, canned pie filling, or preserves)
2 white bread slices

Directions
1. Prepare the campfire.
2. Grease both sides of the pie iron with butter, vegetable oil, or cooking spray.
3. Place one slice of bread at the bottom of the pie iron. Add fruits of your choice. Top with 1 tablespoon of cinnamon-sugar mixture.
4. Place another slice of bread on top. Press down the edges.
5. Close and latch the pie iron.
6. Place the pie iron over the coals and cook on both sides for 2–3 minutes until golden brown.
7. Remove the pie iron from the coals. Serve warm.

Nutrition Facts per Serving
Calories 277, total fat 2.1 g, carb 60.2 g,
Protein 5 g, sodium 422 mg

Cherry Pie

This cheery cherry pie is so easy that even kids can make it. But it does not compromise on deliciousness and always lives up to expectations.

Serves 4 - Prep. time 5 minutes
Cooking time 10 minutes

Ingredients
1 can (21 ounces) cherry pie filling
1 cup whipping cream
8 Crescent Rolls Big N Flaky Pillsbury

Directions
1. Prepare the campfire.
2. Grease both sides of the pie iron with butter, vegetable oil, or cooking spray.
3. Place one roll at the bottom of the pie iron. Add 2 tablespoons of pie filling.
4. Place another roll-on top.
5. Close and latch the pie iron.
6. Place the pie iron over the coals and cook for about 5 minutes. Flip and cook for 5 more minutes until evenly golden.
7. Remove the pie iron from the coals. Serve.

Nutrition Facts per Serving
Calories 559, total fat 23.4 g, carb 80.5 g,
Protein 5.2 g, sodium 697 mg

Pumpkin Pie

Pumpkin pie does not need any sales pitch; this is the one pie that you must make to make the most of your camping trip.

Yield 4 pies - Prep. time 5 minutes
Cooking time 10 minutes

Ingredients
1 cup pumpkin pie filling
4 tablespoon whipping cream (1 tbsp per serving)
8 Flaky Supreme Pillsbury Cinnamon Rolls

Directions
1. Prepare the campfire.
2. Grease both sides of the pie iron with butter, vegetable oil, or cooking spray.
3. Place one roll at the bottom of the pie iron. Add 2 tablespoons of pie filling.
4. Place another roll on top.
5. Close and latch the pie iron.
6. Place the pie iron over the coals and cook for about 5 minutes. Flip and cook for 5 more minutes until evenly golden.
7. Remove the pie iron from the coals. Serve warm with whipped cream on top.

Nutrition Facts per Serving
Calories 368, total fat 16.1 g, carb 52.3 g,
Protein 4.3 g, sodium 725 mg

S'mores Pie

This insanely simple and easy pie recipe will mesmerize you with its aromatic cinnamon and chocolaty flavor. During summer camping trips, s'mores pies are your perfect partner to make up for a hot day's work.

Serves 4 - Prep. time 5 minutes
Cooking time 5 minutes

Ingredients
4 graham cracker squares, crumbled
1 cup mini marshmallows
½ cup chocolate chips
8 slices cinnamon swirl bread

Directions
1. Prepare the campfire.
2. Grease both sides of the pie iron with butter, vegetable oil, or cooking spray.
3. Place one slice of bread at the bottom of the pie iron. Add ¼ of the graham cracker crumbs, 2 tablespoons of the chocolate chips, and ¼ cup of the marshmallows.
4. Place another slice of bread on top.
5. Close and latch the pie iron.
6. Place the pie iron over the coals and cook for about 1 minute. Flip and cook for 1 more minute.
7. Remove the pie iron from the coals. Serve warm.

Nutrition Facts per Serving
Calories 352, total fat 10.7 g, carb 58.2g,
Protein 6.6 g, sodium 326 mg

Chocolate Whoopie Pie

This is a warm and delicious way to fulfill your sweet craving. Kids simply adore these delicious whoopie pies—and so do adults.

Serves 1 - Prep. time 5 minutes - Cooking time 3–5 minutes

Ingredients
Chocolate whoopie pies
Milk chocolate bars, cut into pieces (optional)
Marshmallow cream (optional)
Cold milk to serve

Directions
1. Prepare the campfire.
2. Grease both sides of the pie iron with butter, vegetable oil, or cooking spray.
3. Place a whoopie pie at the bottom of the pie iron. Add some marshmallow cream and chocolate bar pieces.
4. Close and latch the pie iron.
5. Place the pie iron over the coals and cook on both sides until evenly toasted.
6. Remove the pie iron from the coals. Serve warm with cold milk on the side.

Nutrition Facts per Serving
Calories 1343, total fat 32.4 g, carb 248.8 g,
Protein 17.2 g, sodium 586 mg

Apple Pie Cream Dessert

After a long day of exploring, treat your fellow campers with this incredibly creamy apple pie. Make this once and your dessert time will never be the same.

Serves 1 - Prep. time 5 minutes - Cooking time 5 minutes

Ingredients
¼ cup (½ stick) butter, melted
½ cup apple pie filling
2 cups dry white cake mix
2 tablespoons whipped cream or ice cream (optional)

Directions
1. Prepare the campfire.
2. Combine the cake mix and butter in a bowl until well mixed.
3. Add the pie filling and mix. A few visible lumps are okay; do not over-mix.
4. Grease both sides of the pie iron with butter, vegetable oil, or cooking spray.
5. Pour the cake mix into the bottom of the pie iron.
6. Close and latch the pie iron.
7. Place the pie iron over the coals and cook for about 2 minutes. Flip and cook for 2 minutes more.
8. Remove the pie iron from the coals. Serve warm with whipped cream or ice cream.

Nutrition Facts per Serving
Calories 1512, total fat 76.8 g, carb 198.8 g,
Protein 10 g, sodium 1863 mg

Peanut Butter Choco Delight

Who's up for a peanut-butter-perky dessert? Yes, it does have chocolate chips as well!

Serves 1 - Prep. time 5 minutes
Cooking time 5–10 minutes

Ingredients
¼ cup chocolate chips or chocolate bar
1 banana, sliced
2 tablespoons peanut butter
Mini marshmallows
2 slices white bread

Directions
1. Prepare the campfire.
2. Grease both sides of the pie iron with butter, vegetable oil, or cooking spray.
3. Place one slice of bread at the bottom of the pie iron. Spread with peanut butter.
4. Add the chocolate, marshmallows, and bananas. Place another slice of bread on top.
5. Close and latch the pie iron.
6. Place the pie iron over the coals and cook for about 2–3 minutes per side until crisp.
7. Remove the pie iron from the coals. Serve.

Nutrition Facts per Serving
Calories 844, total fat 45.6 g, carb 95.6 g,
Protein 22.9 g, sodium 471 mg

RECIPE INDEX

BREAKFAST

SANDWICHES AND BREAD

PIZZAS AND PIES

CAMPING MEALS

DESSERTS AND COOKIES

APPENDIX
COOKING CONVERSION CHARTS

1. Measuring Equivalent Chart

Type	Imperial	Imperial	Metric
Weight	1 dry ounce		28g
	1 pound	16 dry ounces	0.45 kg
Volume	1 teaspoon		5 ml
	1 dessert spoon	2 teaspoons	10 ml
	1 tablespoon	3 teaspoons	15 ml
	1 Australian tablespoon	4 teaspoons	20 ml
	1 fluid ounce	2 tablespoons	30 ml
	1 cup	16 tablespoons	240 ml
	1 cup	8 fluid ounces	240 ml
	1 pint	2 cups	470 ml
	1 quart	2 pints	0.95 l
	1 gallon	4 quarts	3.8 l
Length	1 inch		2.54 cm

*   Numbers are rounded to the closest equivalent

2. Oven Temperature Equivalent Chart

Fahrenheit (°F)	Celsius (°C)	Gas Mark
220	100	
225	110	1/4
250	120	1/2
275	140	1
300	150	2
325	160	3
350	180	4
375	190	5
400	200	6
425	220	7
450	230	8
475	250	9
500	260	

* Celsius (°C) = T (°F)-32] * 5/9

** Fahrenheit (°F) = T (°C) * 9/5 + 32

*** Numbers are rounded to the closest equivalent

Printed in Great Britain
by Amazon

40195611R00046